I0462979

Get Your Greeting Cards Into Stores

How to Find and Work with Sales Reps

Kate Harper

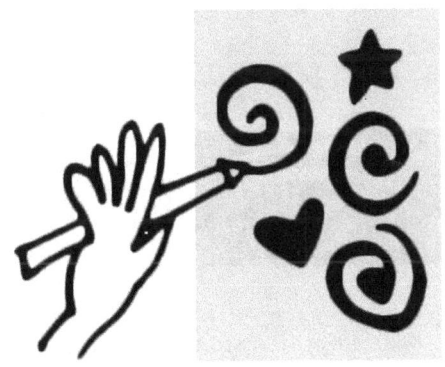

Copyright © 2017, ©2024 Kate Harper All rights reserved.

ISBN-10: 1461132134
ISBN-13: 978-1461132134

DEDICATION

To Ginger McCleskey,
who helps artists
get through the forest.

CONTENTS

Go to the places that scare you!

-Milarepa, Tibetan Yogi

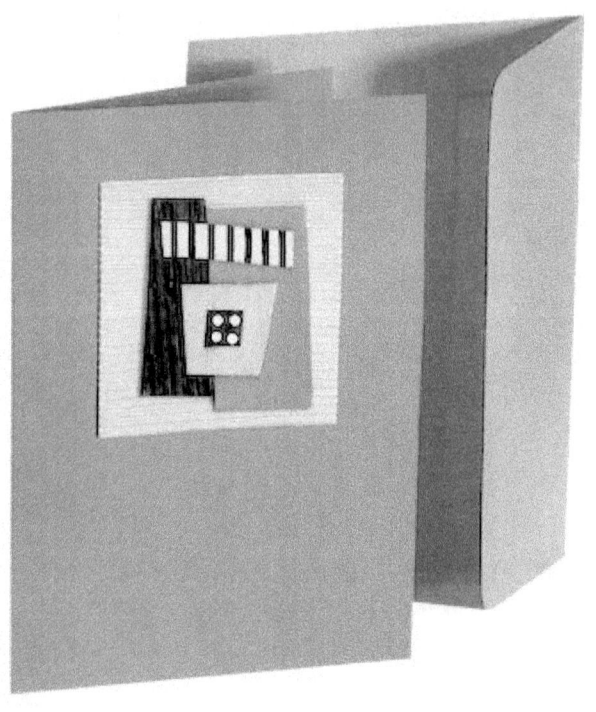

INTRODUCTION

For fifteen years, I published and sold my handmade greeting cards to over 2,000 accounts, including national chains, bookstores, grocery stores, airport gift shops, and even car washes.

From all my experience, I continue to believe the greeting card business is still one of the few businesses a person can start at home on the kitchen table. Even though today more people communicate through digital media rather than mailing letters, I still see new indie artists entering the business and succeeding, especially 'handmade' card designers.

If you publish your own cards, there are some positive trends leaning your way. Since most sales statistics for the greeting card industry are based on figures from large corporations, it is hard to know what is really going on in the smaller, independent greeting card market.

To find out what is happening I interviewed several independently owned gift stores. I asked them what trends they see in the card market and I was surprised that they all reported an increase in sales.

When I asked them to respond to negative news articles I'd seen about national greeting card sales, they mostly felt those statistics did not apply to them.

They reported that cards are a popular item. They do the best with more artistic, handmade, and local artist's cards and attribute it to the fact that "people want to touch paper again."

One store reported that it was common for a customer to come to the register with $35-$40 worth of cards, and they buy cards because they like a particular art style or theme (and not necessarily because they need greeting cards).

All stores said they served a completely different market than chain stores that carry greeting cards. One manager reported, "People who buy cards in our store, take time to evaluate them. People who are just running errands or need to buy a card out of an obligation, tend to buy cards in drugstore chains."

Here are some trends they reported:

- Customers are willing to spend over $5 per card.

- Younger "hipster" buyers are coming into the market.

- Customers will buy cards to keep, and frame for inspiration.

- Customers often ask for help when selecting a card and they want to know "the story" behind the publisher or the artist.

• Cards are not always mailed, but are instead given by hand, person to person.

Almost every store emphasized that their customers buy cards for the imagery, and not for text. Trends are shifting to "thought-provoking" imagery that makes the customer ask, "what is this about?" An example that was shown to me was a picture of a moose riding a bicycle. Surprisingly, all the top selling cards in all of the stores I interviewed did not have text on them.

I asked store managers what artists should do if they want to succeed in the card business today. Here are their suggestions:

• Pay special attention to your image. It is more important than it used to be.

• Witty text isn't necessary. Leaving it blank or just saying "happy birthday" is good enough.

• Create more cards that can be bought any day of the year, and not limit them to one occasion.

• Make cards that are curious and unpredictable.

• If you are just starting out, create Birthday, Thank You, Valentine's Day and blank cards (no words).

While my informal interviews were limited to Northern California, some of the responses were also consistent with the National Procurement Report of the greeting card industry. This report stated that overall corporate card sales were down, but that *"...areas of growth are likely small geographic locations, and niches in the market."*

This is all good news for card designers in the age of technology. Rather than rely on news reports or business analysts, the most accurate information is from the source: The retail store. I encourage all designers to not be shy. Ask your local independent gift retailer the same questions that I did.

~

When I started making cards, I didn't know how to get them into retail stores, nor did I understand how the greeting card business worked. I spent time learning about the industry, sought out advice, welcomed criticism and went back to the drawing board several times to solve problems and create new designs.

Because of my years of experience, I often get emails from artists who want advice. The most common question they ask me is "How can I get my cards into stores?" In this book, I will answer that question and more.

Even though this book is about greeting cards, the information is also applicable to all gift items, including magnets, journals, calendars, collectibles, etc. This is because the gift industry and greeting card industry are similar. Stores who buy cards often buy gifts.

The suggestions in this book are a result of my personal experience as an artist. For every piece of advice I offer, another artist or publisher might do things differently, which points to the fact that there is no one "right way" to run a card business. This is why I like this business. There is flexibility to do things your own way.

For example, some people believe it is essential to exhibit at industry trade shows, which can be quite expensive for an independent artist. I tend to discourage this, especially for beginners, because they don't guarantee orders or new accounts.

I believe the best way to grow a card business is to work with independent greeting card sales representatives, (also called "reps"). These are professionals in the greeting card industry who sell cards to retail stores.

Why Artists Like to Work With Reps

Besides generating orders, there are many benefits to working with reps. Here are just a few:

- You Get Quick Access to Stores.
  Reps offer fast entry into the marketplace. Once a rep has a sample set of your card line, they can start showing it to stores immediately.

- Reps Can Sell More Than Artists Can.

Reps usually have years of sales experience and personal relationships with hundreds of stores. Therefore, a rep is able to sell many more cards than an artist could.

• Reps Know What the Store Wants.
Reps know the store owner's personality, what kind of products they like, and what types of customers visit each store. Reps build bridges between the artist, the store, and the customer.

• Reps Are Industry Experts.
Sales reps have valuable information on buying trends and can advise an artist to explore new directions.

• Working With Reps Help Reduce Risk.
An artist can avoid a financial risk if they have several independent reps throughout the country. For example, if you put your entire card line in the hands of one store chain or distributor, and later they drop you, your business will end overnight. On the other hand, if you lose one sales rep, it is only a temporary setback until you find a replacement.

• Reps Provide Cost Savings.
One of the biggest advantages of working with sales reps, is you only need to pay a commission on what cards are sold. You are not paying a salary. This is a flexible and low cost way to generate sales.

• You Can Avoid Regulations.

Another benefit of working with reps is because they are commission-based, you don't have to follow employee regulations as you would for an employee, such workman's comp payments.

- Reps are Invested in the Artist's Success
  When a rep decides to carry a card line, they have made a personal investment in your success. They have confidence the cards will sell. It is a win–win for everyone.

Why Stores Like to Work with Reps

There are several reasons why stores also like to work with reps:

- Reps Offer Unique Products
  Reps are often good at finding specialty items, which gives smaller stores an edge over large chain stores.

- Reps Save the Stores Time
  Stores save time by viewing many card lines in one appointment. This is more efficient than requesting catalogs from multiple individual artists and manufacturers.

- Reps Bring Samples
  Another advantage for the store is they can hold items in their hands and evaluate it, instead of guessing the quality when ordering online or through a catalog.

- Reps Prescreen Items
  Lastly, stores trust reps to prescreen quality card lines, which reduces financial risk for the store. If a card line does not sell very well, a rep will be hesitant to carry it, and this protects the store from financial losses.

In order to find and work with sales reps, you need to consider doing these three things:

1) Get professional feedback on your designs.
2) Set appropriate prices.
3) Follow industry standards.

We will discuss these in the next several chapters.

Starting At the Kitchen Table

When starting out, it's good to experiment with selling your cards in alternative venues such as local craft fairs and online websites such as Etsy www.etsy.com . These are places to get direct feedback from customers. You might find people prefer your dog images over your flower images, or your humor themes over your sentimental themes.

I sold my first cards to a roommate. Friends and relatives also bought my cards, and I even created wedding invitations. I sold at craft fairs and even at a yard sale once! These examples may sound simplistic, but they were important stages of the business.

I soon realized that selling cards in these kinds of venues was helpful and fun, but it was also a limited market - because I could only sell a few cards at a time. I wanted to see if I could sell enough cards to actually make a living. But before making that leap, I sought out professional advice and feedback on my designs. Getting feedback was probably the most important thing I did at this point. Don't be afraid to ask for brutal honesty! It can point you toward the direction of success.

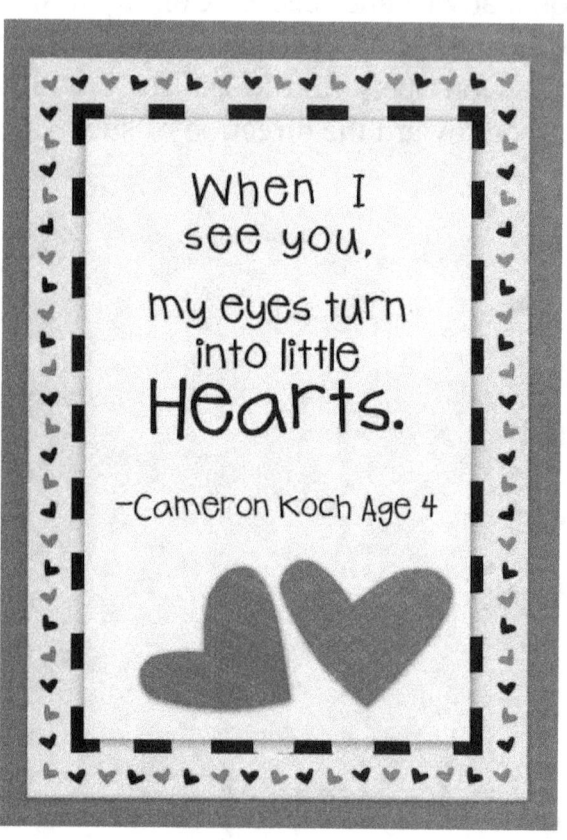

When I see you,

my eyes turn into little

Hearts.

—Cameron Koch Age 4

CHAPTER 1
GETTING FEEDBACK

Once you create a line of cards (perhaps 24-36), it is important to have a professional evaluate your designs. You can probably find someone in your community, such as a store owner.

Here are some suggestions of ways you can get feedback. I tried all of these ideas, and it was easy to do because all the people lived in my local community.

Ask a Store to Meet with Artists

I asked a manager of a greeting card store if she would be willing to advise me (and some friends) about how to make good greeting card designs. She met with us after closing time, looked at our cards, and answered our questions. She told us which occasions sold well (birthday), what colors to avoid (black and white) and why we should design in a vertical format instead of horizontal (more cards fit on a shelf).

We were grateful she spent her free time helping us, but our meeting was just as important to her. She didn't realize her knowledge and skills were valuable to artists. Normally, her days involved managing staff, unpacking boxes, and stocking card racks. Meeting with us was a breath of fresh air - to do something different. She also learned how much she knew about cards. She didn't realize it until she found herself answering so many of our questions!

Approach the Grinch

I walked by a tiny bookstore many times, trying to get up the courage to walk in and ask the owner to look at my cards. His personality was a little like the Grinch, which was intimidating, but it turned out he wasn't the Grinch at all. He did offer brutally honest advice. He explained to me why no one in his store would buy my cards (ouch!), but then proceeded to place an order for several dozen! That was a surprise. Perhaps he was just giving me a chance to see if he was correct, or not correct.

Take a Class

Look around in your community for greeting card classes. I found one at my local adult school

During class, the teacher told a story of how he left his corporate sales career and started a card business with a partner. Since he came from a business background, and not from a design background, his view of the card business was numbers and formulas.

After his lecture, I showed him my handmade cards and the first thing he said to me was *"you need to change these designs so that other people can make them. You cannot grow a card business if you are the only person making your cards."*

That was somewhat of a shock to hear, but a great piece of advice. After that, I completely changed the designs so that other people, besides me, could make them.

Attend a Supplier-wholesaler Local Event

One day I received an invitation to a seminar sponsored by a local paper company, possibly because I ordered some paper and swatch books earlier in the year. I decided to attend out of curiosity. When I arrived, I was surprised to meet a well known greeting card designer. It was a great opportunity to ask for advice.

Think about all the materials you use and what supplies you buy locally. Ask for a tour, an informational meeting, and bring your friends.

Write to an Artist

Once I bought a handmade card by a local artist and decided to write to her because I loved her cards. I also sent her some of my cards, and asked if I could get advice on how to improve them. Since her cards were a completely different style from mine, I felt it was OK to contact her. Not only did she help me, but she also invited me to her studio and answered many more of my questions.

Ask a Sales Rep

Consider attending a wholesale gift show that exhibits many wares by different artists and manufacturers. You might be able to meet a sales representative in an exhibitor's booth. Rather than talking in the booth and interrupting sales, ask her if you could take her out to lunch in exchange for giving feedback.

I did this, thinking to myself: *What is the worst that can happen?* All she can do is say 'no'. But luckily, she said yes.

Greeting card sales representatives are one of the best resources for feedback. They see a variety of products and often have a gut sense about trends and what will sell.

Since artists often approach reps, it is nice to offer them something for their time, such as taking them out to lunch or even paying for their time as a consultant. They usually have a very busy schedule; so, tell them up front you will limit your meeting to an hour. If they decide to stay longer, then great, you can too. Alternatively, if they only have 5 minutes, that is still enough time to get some basic advice.

These are only a few ideas of how you might get feedback on your cards. If you cannot find anyone to get advice from, consider paying a professional greeting card consultant or to get peer-to-peer advice through social networks of people in the greeting card business (See "Resources" section).

A card consultant is an expert who works in the stationery industry and can help manufacturers and designers. They do everything from: helping you plan for trade shows, to giving you specific design tips to improve sales. They have seen many card lines succeed and fail, and they are aware of emerging trends. It might be worth a few hundred dollars just to have them look at your cards.

If the consultant lives in another state and meeting in person is not possible, they will often arrange for you to email or mail card samples ahead of time, and then do a consultation over the phone or by video.

Get On-the-Spot Feedback

If you are unable to get a formal appointment for feedback, try to visit at least six stores and ask for feedback on-the-spot. Here's how:

Visit a store during slow times, such as a weekday morning. If a store employee is not busy, ask them if the "card buyer" would be willing to give you five minutes for some honest feedback on your designs. Explain that you are not trying to sell anything; you just want to improve your cards to make them more marketable.

Remember, there are *different kinds of staff people* in the store. The person running the cash register may not be the person who buys cards or is qualified to evaluate designs, so always make sure you ask for the "card buyer." More often than not, they will come onto the floor to assist you.

If the card buyer has a positive response to your cards, ask for a price recommendation. Perhaps they know what a good price is for your cards. If all you do is walk away with a page full of notes and information, that is a complete success.

In a situation where you only want feedback, it's also possible the store might want to try out your cards in their store, so bring an order form, brochure, or business card, just in case.

If the above scenarios sound scary and you don't like walking up to strangers and asking for things, then just try it once and see what happens. I have done this many times, and not once did anyone treat me rudely or act irritated. I consistently had good experiences, and people were happy to help me. But I also made sure to respect their time and not interrupt them if they were assisting customers. I also sent a thank you card.

These "on-the-spot" requests for feedback are a great way to meet local buyers who can also refer you to reps, vendors, and other professionals in the industry.

Use Social Media

Another way to get feedback on your card line is to establish relationships with people who work in the greeting card industry through social media. You can do this by connecting through LinkedIn, Google+, Yahoo Groups, Twitter, Facebook and other social networks.

You can ask questions directly to people who work in the industry and discuss specific topics. In most cases, you can also post images of your designs. I've often posted cards and asked people to vote on which design they like the best.

Here are some social media groups to consider:

Greeting Card Designer Facebook Page
This is a private facebook group for artists, writers and other professionals in the greeting card business. A great place for beginners to get support and feedback. www.facebook.com/groups/greetingcarddesigner

Greeting Card, Stationery & Gift Industry Gurus
This is a greeting card network focused on sales, marketing, and product development, to help entrepreneurs gain access to industry knowledge and 'how to's." www.linkedin.com/groups/950007

Stationery Trends Facebook Page
This is the Facebook group of the magazine "Stationery Trends." Its focus is on products in the stationery, greeting card, and gift industry.
www.facebook.com/StationeryTrends

Greeting Card Association Facebook Page
The Greeting Card Association (GCA) is the U.S.-based trade organization representing greeting card and stationery publishers, and related industries..
www.facebook.com/GreetingCardAssociation

National Stationery Show Facebook Page

This group attracts buyers from stationery, card and gift shops, and even including bookstores, bridal shops, and party stores. They also service chain and "big box" mass retailers, as well as importers and distributors.
www.facebook.com/NationalStationeryShow

Make and Appointment with Experts

Whether you wander into a bookstore on a whim or decide to set up a formal meeting with a paid professional, all these people have the skills of a professional consultant. Anyone who sells, designs, or works in the greeting card industry can be of great help in your design development.

I refer to all these people collectively as "consultants," since they have industry information.

Unlike friends and family, a greeting card consultant can offer professional advice on how to make your cards marketable on a wider scale. They also have connections in the industry. This kind of information is priceless.

I believe that in order to grow a successful card business, it is probably better to get advice from a store "Grinch" rather than your grandma!

What to Do in a One-on-One Meeting

If possible, try to arrange a meeting in a location where neither of you will be interrupted. Meeting in a cafe is even more desirable than meeting at a work site, because when someone is at work (such as a buyer in a bookstore), their staff can often pull them away to help attend to something in the store.

Here are some guidelines on how to prepare for a meeting with a consultant:

- Bring a notebook and write down what they say, whether positive or negative.

- Bring your greeting cards as a finished product with an envelope, as if you were ready to present them to a store. This helps the consultant visualize what your cards will look like on a card rack. If your cards are handmade, consider packaging each one individually in a cellophane bag. This will help prevent embellishments from falling off, or images from getting smeared by handling.

- Keep your cards loose. Avoid putting them in a photo album or portfolio. Consultants generally want to shuffle through cards, sort them into piles, and look at the backside. If the cards are restricted to an album format, none of these tasks can be easily performed.

- Try to bring at least two dozen different card designs to the meeting. Three dozen is good, and five dozen is even better! By showing a range of designs, the consultant can offer a direction. But if you only show one dozen cards, it may be hard to see your vision or potential.

• Number the cards. Adhere a sticker to the back of each card and identify individual designs. You can name them, use letters, or any other identifier. It's much easier to refer to "card #7" when taking notes, rather than "the card with a red flower and orangish middle."

• During the meeting, try to emotionally separate yourself from your art. Encourage the consultant up front to be brutally honest with you. Assure them they will not hurt your feelings. You could even pretend your cards belong to someone else. That way, it will be easier for you to listen.

Tips for Getting Helpful Information

• Ask the consultant to put your cards into piles by preference. You can make it very simple, such as:

(1) Cards they think could sell.
(2) Cards they don't think would sell (or "rejected").
(3) Cards that might be improved with a small change.

• Regarding the rejected cards, ask them to be specific about what the problem is with each card, and how it could be improved.

• After they create piles, don't forget which pile they *don't* like! Put the "rejected" cards in a bag, out of the way, so you avoid remixing them with the rest of your cards. Otherwise, when you get home you might forget which ones were accepted and which ones were rejected.

• When asking for feedback, specify you are asking for which ones they think would *sell*, versus which ones they like. This allows three things to happen:

   (1) It's easier for the consultant to be honest about the card's selling potential, rather than be distracted by which ones they personally like.

   (2) It makes it easier for them to reject "the card" instead of "the artist." Reps often have positive and upbeat personalities, and they don't want the artist to feel criticized personally.

   (3) It shows you are a businessperson, and are primarily interested in making a successful product that sells, versus it being a hobby.

• If you are presenting several different styles, ask if they could foresee developing a larger line around one of one of the styles. For example, if you have 12 collage cards, 12 letterpress cards and 12 humor cards, ask which style you should expand to 50 cards.

• Ask them to comment aloud on their first reaction to each card. You might even hand them cards in a specific order that corresponds to a checklist you brought. Then you can take notes on each card while they comment.

• As with most business interactions, it is always nice

to send a thank you note after a meeting. It's possible that in the future they might refer you to other people, including sales reps.

When getting feedback, try not to lose sight of the bigger picture: You are asking for advice on improvement. Come to the meeting prepared they might say your entire line has a problem. But it's also possible they see only one thing to change, such as the text, color or size. It's better to know this information early on, rather than spend $1,000 on materials that might end up sitting in your basement.

A consultant may not like your line because they aren't familiar with your product category. For example, if you make upscale handmade cards, but their specialty is mass-produced cards for drugstores, they may not have experience with the handmade card market.

Taking all of these suggestions into consideration, remember that one consultant is only one opinion. It helps to hear from five or six people. These six people can be store owners, sales reps, or anyone who works in the greeting card industry.

If at this point, you decide that adapting and changing your cards is not the direction you want to go, and you were happier making cards just for friends, that's OK. It's better to know now, rather than later, after you invest time and money in starting a business. However, if at this point you feel energized and interested in making your cards more marketable to the public, then you are probably ready to start a card business. At this point, the next step is to test market your cards.

Do Test Marketing

Ultimately, the best feedback you can get is from the customers who are actually shopping in a store. Don't dismiss the possibility of giving cards away to a store for a limited amount of time in exchange for temporary shelf space for test marketing. You mainly want to know if customers will buy your cards, and how much they are willing to pay.

If a store is hesitant to experiment with your cards because they don't want to give up retail space to an untested product, agree to remove your cards after a month. There is no harm in asking. All they can do is say "no, thanks."

If you feel shy about walking into a store and asking, "Hey, can I put my cards in your store as an experiment?" you have some options:

Talk to your friends or relatives to see if they know anyone who runs a retail store. Tell them you are willing to give away cards in exchange for shelf space for a test market.

I found my first store this way. My friend's mom ran a health food store and she offered to put my cards in a basket on the counter. She took an interest in my success and reported back to me about the customers' comments.

What makes this a great deal for the store is they get

free cards, 100% profit, and they don't have to keep track of invoices or set up an account with you.

I suggest offering at least fifty cards. If that seems expensive to you, remember that when you grow a business, you will often give out free samples to sales reps. So, giving away cards is a common thing to do.

Remember: Stores like artists. In my experience of approaching card buyers, I found them to be generous and helpful. They like giving feedback and usually prefer carrying local artist's products, rather than being limited to mass-marketed items carried in chain stores.

CHAPTER 2
GETTING YOUR FIRST ACCOUNT

If you receive positive feedback from consultants or test marketing, you are ready to try and sell your cards to stores.

Getting store accounts is an important step on the way to getting sales reps. Reps often want to know if your cards are already selling in stores, before they take your line. It's a bit like a catch 22: You need reps in order to sell to stores, but reps look for lines that are already selling in the store.

At this point, it's helpful to know some basic business skills. There is a false stereotype that artists are bad at business, and I like to joke that there are a lot more business people who are bad at art. Therefore, you are actually ahead of the game.

I believe if you do the following tasks, you will be good at running a business. These might sound like common sense items, but stores have told me many times, that card artists neglect them:

• Ship orders on time.

• Send the correct items.

• Charge the correct price.

• Do not add excessive shipping charges.

• Make sure the cards are packaged so they arrive undamaged and without bent corners.

• If cards do arrive damaged, replace them immediately at no extra charge. (I even like to add extra free cards to offset their hassle of requesting replacements.)

• Make sure the cards match the quality of the samples. If the samples had yellow envelopes, make sure all the cards shipped have the same envelope color.

• Include a packing slip in the box (a list of all the items that should be in the box).

• Mail an invoice (bill).

By performing these simple tasks, it shows that you are a reliable, responsible, and action-oriented businessperson.

Adding Stores

When adding more store accounts, add them slowly. This

will help you ramp up your manufacturing and deal with problems that might arise in the future.

For example, when I started selling cards, I kept envelopes in the garage and soon found out the dampness caused the flaps to stick together. I discovered that packing cards tightly caused the cellophane bags to stick together because they could not "breathe." Later on, I also discovered the special Japanese paper I relied on was discontinued, and I needed to find a new supplier.

It's easier to deal with these unexpected supply problems when servicing just a few stores, rather than a hundred. Otherwise, you will get complaints and returns, and that can reflect badly on your business, both in the eyes of the store and the rep. You particularly need to be careful when using unusual supplies that are hard to find. This is why starting with just a few stores is a good idea.

If you find you can handle more growth, consider working towards having at least fifty good-selling designs, and removing the slower sellers from your card line. I think it's better to offer fewer cards with great designs that sell, rather than a hundred cards of questionable quality.

When you feel you have a solid card line and several store accounts, you are probably ready to approach reps, but don't be surprised if reps start contacting you first, especially if your cards are in stores selling well.

This points to the best way to find reps: Create a product that sells, and everything else will fall into place.

Reps just magically appear!

Getting Reorders

To evaluate card sales, reorders are more important than first orders. A reorder means a customer walked into the store and bought your cards, which requires the store to *restock the shelf.*

However, first orders only mean the store bought your cards and put them on the shelf. This does not guarantee customers will buy them. This is referred to as the "sell-through" rate, or the percentage of cards that actually end up being purchased by customers.

For most reps, knowing that one store reordered your cards ten times is much more impressive than knowing ten stores bought your cards once, but did not reorder.

CHAPTER 3
PRICING AND PROFITS

Selling to retail stores is very different from selling to individual customers at craft fairs. Stores usually buy larger quantities, and for wholesale prices.

If you normally sell your cards for $4 each at a craft fair, you cannot expect a retail store to buy them for the same price. Stores need to make a profit, which requires them to double the price at which they buy them.

It may be unrealistic to expect a store to just double your $4 price and sell your cards for $8. Unless your cards are very unusual or have detachable gifts, the average consumer may not purchase a card in that price range. Therefore, it's helpful to evaluate your costs, look at your profits. and reexamine your manufacturing process. You and the store *both* need to make money!

Even though your profit "per card" is smaller when you sell at a wholesale price, you have the ability to sell large quantities. A store might order two hundred cards and reorder quarterly. Therefore, it is better to sell large volumes of cards to several stores for a lower price than to sell a few cards at a craft fair for a higher price.

Sometimes artists get so excited about getting their cards into stores, they neglect to look at the cost of making cards. You want to know early on you will make a profit. Six months down the road, you don't want to find out you are working for ten cents an hour. If you suddenly quit the business because you are not making any money, it's not fair to you, the store, or the rep. It's important to make sure all your numbers add up, before you look for a rep.

Determining Materials Costs

The greeting card business has many types of costs, but the biggest one is usually the materials costs. Materials are the physical supplies used to make your cards, such as glue, paint, cellophane bags, envelopes, and paper. If it cannot be "touched," and is not a part of the card, it is not a material cost. A shipping label is not a materials cost because it is not part of the actual greeting card.

When determining materials costs, disassemble your finished card, and make a list of all the parts, including things like a spot of glue, an envelope, paper and ink. Determine how much each item costs per card. If your cards are printed, you might only have two costs: The printed card and the envelope.

It's easy to have your heart set on one specific type of paper for your cards, but if the cost is too high, be flexible. Sales reps have often told me that artists tend to be overly picky about things that stores and customers don't really care about, such as how thick an envelope is, or what kind of paper the card is printed on.

Profitability Formula

As a rule of thumb, I have found that if you make 20 to 25 percent profit on each card, then you are doing great! These percentages are based on wholesale prices. For example, if I sell my cards to a store for $1.50 each, my goal is to make a profit of at least 20 percent (or 30 cents) on each card.

Use these guidelines below to evaluate your costs. If they don't match, look at where you can make adjustments by using less expensive materials or changing the design. Do you really need three pieces of paper glued on, or can you get away with just having two? Do you really need a deckled edge envelope, or can you use a plain one?

Aim for the following numbers. Pretend they are different parts of a pie, and you need to put them together to total 100 percent. If you sell cards at a different price, substitute your number (in place of the $1.50) and ratio.

- Try to make your materials cost between 15 to 35 percent "of the pie" (22-52 cents for card that is $1.50)

- Allow 10 to 20 percent for labor if you are hand making the card, or need hand assembly. (15-30 cents).

- Your office costs (shipping, labels, invoices, etc) may be about 10 to 20 percent of pie (15-30 cents).

- Allow 20 percent of the 1.50 for a sales representative (30 cents).

- Aim for 20 percent or more, for your profit (30 cents).

If you can only ask one question, ask this one: "If I sold as many cards as I wanted, would I make enough money to be happy?"

Alternatively, you can break this down into the following questions:

- After my expenses are deducted, how much profit do I make per card?

- How much money am I making per hour?

- If sales doubled next month and I need to pay someone to help me, can I afford it?

The Tale of Two Businesses:

When growing a card business, only purchase items that are absolutely necessary. Avoid the enticement of pseudo-business expenses, like tax deductible perks.

For example, imagine these somewhat humorous scenarios. Which card business would you rather have?

Business #1

You are sitting in your rented sunlit art studio with your new computer, loaded with the latest software, and you have just returned from the art supply store to see what fun things you could buy. Earlier in the day, you stopped by the Chamber of Commerce to buy a ticket to a networking dinner at the local country club.

Then you sat down to add up your monthly bills, and were surprised to find that you were spending $2,000 a month on your business, but all the receipts have nothing to do with making a greeting card. Rather, they are for rent, business lunches, a new drafting table, art books and business cards.

The next day, when you share this information with your spouse (partner, kid, wife, mother, etc), they say, "This hobby of yours is too expensive. I think you need to give it up. We could have used that $2,000 to pay for the rent (braces, gas, insurance, food, etc)."

Business #2

Instead of the Chamber of Commerce network event, you just had coffee with some people in your neighborhood who work at home. You learned one neighbor needs invitations for her daughter's wedding, and another tells you about Freecycle www.freecycle.org, where people give away things they don't need.

You scored a free drafting table and a bunch of cardboard boxes and mailing labels.

At the end of the month, you added your sales and found you profited $2,000. You share this information with your family and they are happy for you. Your spouse (partner, kid, wife, mother) suggests moving the exercise bike out of the spare room and into the garage, and then you turn the workout room into an art room.

Because your business is profitable, you can grow and purchase larger quantities of supplies for cheaper, bulk discounts. You have very little overhead costs and   it's easier to grow the business.

~

When I first started my card business, I had many difficulties with sales.   When downturns came, I was tempted to think my business was just something I dabbled at while working a full time job.   I got more advice, made adjustments, and I eventually found there were more ups than there were downs.

If you feel like you are on a roller coaster, that is normal. Any good business generally starts that way, and things change as you go along. My biggest piece of advice for dealing with this is: If you start feeling disappointed, take action.:Ask for advice. Make adjustments. Work on new ideas. Do something. Don't just give up because you had a bad day or someone criticized your art.

If someone criticized the quality of your essay on a college exam, you wouldn't just quit school, would you? The greeting card business is no different. You still need to do research, do the homework, and ask for feedback.

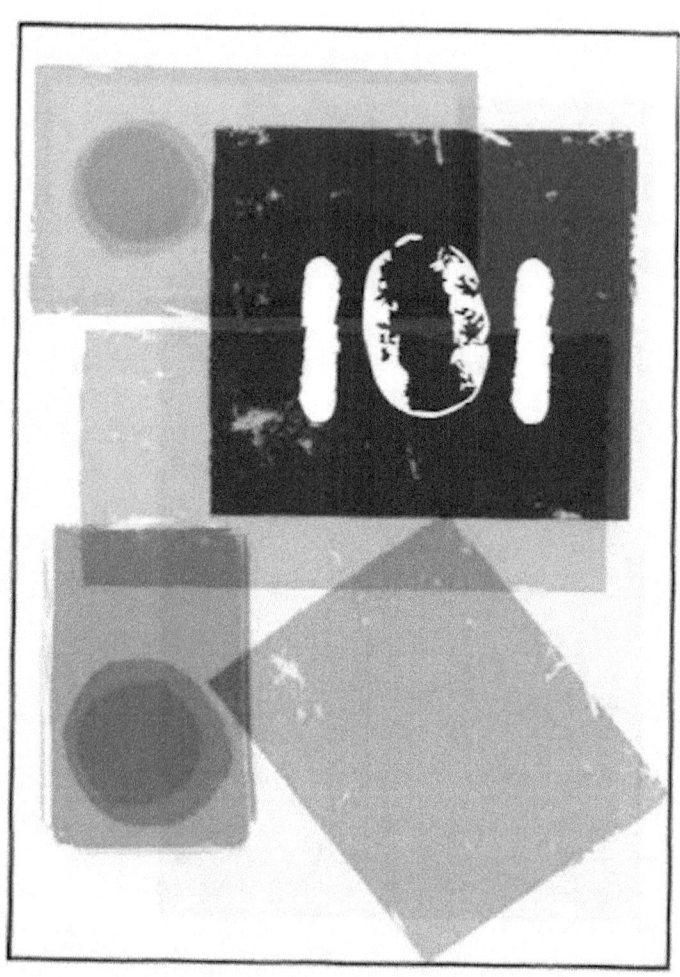

CHAPTER 4
SALES REPS 101

There are many benefits of starting small, getting your cards into stores, before looking for a rep. If you rush to get one, and then find out your card line doesn't sell well, reps might tell other reps and then it can be hard to get a second rep. Even if you make dramatic changes to your line, you could still end up living in the shadows of outdated information circulating around about your cards.

I learned this after creating three lines. The first two flopped, and the third one succeeded. I'm glad I didn't try to expand my business early on, because several reps would have experienced my failures with me. Then I would have gained a reputation as "the artist with the crummy line"! However, because I waited until I had a good line before I added reps, they did not experience my first two flops!

On the other end of the spectrum, nothing travels faster than good news. If your line sells well, reps will start contacting you out of nowhere. When I got an account with a national bookstore chain, I had a dozen reps call me, asking if they could carry my line. I didn't know any of these reps, but they were aware of me because they saw my cards appear on the store shelves in their local stores. They told other reps who worked in adjacent territories.

What Reps Do

A rep's primary responsibility is to sell cards. She (most are women) makes appointments with store card buyers and shows samples made by artists and publishers (collectively called "manufacturers").

Besides your cards, she might carry dozens of other card lines by a variety of artists, along with gift products such as mugs, candles, magnets, or calendars. The store purchases the cards, the rep writes the order on the spot, and then sends you the order. You are then responsible for shipping the cards to the store, and collecting the payment. The store pays the artist, but the artist is the one who pays the rep.

If a rep brings ten different card lines (of ten different manufactures) into a meeting, and each line has one hundred different card designs, a buyer could easily see one thousand cards in a single meeting. But the rep does not want to overwhelm the buyer with too many products at once, so she may limit the number of items viewed at a given meeting. She might show Valentine's cards in one meeting, and birthday cards a few months later.

Other things a rep often does is: travel long distances, carry heavy boxes of samples, and straighten display racks. A good rep builds relationships. She is reliable and on time, is aware of community issues, and often possesses a congenial personality. She is also extremely skilled at finding parking spaces!

An artist rarely sees these activities from a distance, yet they are vital skills that help you grow your business.

There is no comparable advertising investment, online site, mobile technology, trade show, or marketing strategy that can do what reps do. It is nearly impossible to perform all of these functions without physically being in a store. Luckily, there are thousands of greeting card reps throughout the United States who do this.

Independent Reps versus In-house Reps

While I mainly worked with independent reps who ran their own businesses, there is another type of rep called an "in-house" rep. In-house reps are usually full-time salaried employees who work primarily for one card company. They do not generally carry lines by independent artists. I am only going to discuss "independent reps", and not in-house reps, but it is good to know about them just in case you hear the term and wonder what it means.

Larger publishers might have both types of reps. Sometimes your card line and large publisher might have the same rep because the larger company cannot afford a full time sales person for a specific territory. Sometimes this can benefit you if the reps are visiting stores the bigger company sells to.

Getting Technical: What is a Card Line Anyway?

Once you start working with sales reps, you might find the term "card line" has multiple meanings. The simplest definition is: a set of greeting cards by one manufacturer. Let us assume you are an artist from New York who has created 50 different photo cards of cats and dogs. You call this business "New York Pets." Then you meet a rep and she decides to "pick up" your line, or add it to her collection. She asks you to give her one sample of each card (of your 50 card designs). These 50 card samples are often called "a deck," like a deck of cards. This is one meaning of the word "card line."

Another description of a card line can also refer to a group of cards with a specific "style." One artist can have several different styles. Using the same example above, perhaps you decide to add magnets; you might call them the "pet magnet line." Then later you add another greeting card line called "New York birds." Your New York Pet card line has a new "bird line." Therefore, a "line" can mean different things depending on the context.

Usually a rep needs one sample of each item in your line. For a magnet line, she needs a sample of each magnet, and for a candle line, she might also need a sample of each candle. Whether or not the rep totes heavy items around, that is her choice. In a store appointment, she may opt to only bring one candle with a catalog of photos of the other candles, but she should have the option to request a sample of every item in your line.

CHAPTER 5
WHERE TO FIND REPS

I jokingly call greeting card reps - the "underground sales network." They do not have a professional association, a directory, or group website, and it can be hard to find them. Most of the reps I have met, I found simply through personal contacts. But if you do not know how to find a rep, here are some different ways to find them, starting with the easiest way.

Ask Stores

Stores know many reps, so ask them for a referral. They may hesitate if you do not already sell to their store, because they don't want to give personal information to a stranger. But if you do sell to the store already, stores are generally willing to help you out. If you sell to an out of state store that is hard to visit, you can offer incentives for their rep recommendations.

For example, if you live in California and your sister in Minnesota helped you get your cards into her local store, this is a great opportunity to ask that store buyer for recommendations on local reps. In a case like this, you can offer the store two dozen free cards if they help you find a rep in their territory. This system worked great for me, especially in remote areas where reps are hard to find.

The best thing about doing this, is when you contact the rep the very first time, you can say "Abby's gift store recommended you" versus "Hi, I'm an artist looking for a rep." Most likely, the rep already knows Abby's store, and values their recommendation over the many artists who contact them out of the blue and have no relationship to a local store.

Put Contact Information on the Back of Your Cards

Reps sometimes found me by reading the contact information from the backside of my cards. Reps visit hundreds of stores, even ones outside of their own territory or while on vacation. Remember to put contact information on your cards that will be valid in the future. Greeting cards have a tendency to float around for years and end up on people's bulletin boards or in filing cabinets. Periodically I still receive messages from people who just discovered one of my cards printed ten years ago. Luckily, my email address was still valid!

Reps Recommend other Other Reps

Once you have a rep and your line sells well, that rep will tell other reps. They have contacts and friendships with colleagues in different states and territories, and they often refer lines to each other as a favor or exchange of information.

Search Online

If a rep has a website, sometimes they will have contact information and artist submission guidelines.

Always read their website to see if your cards would fit into their lines. And also look around for a link topic such as "Artists" or "submission guidelines." These pages will give you updated information on whether they are looking for new lines, and how to submit your products for them to review.

Ask for Referrals on LinkedIn

Many sales reps are active on social networks. They might be members of groups such as the LinkedIn Group: Greeting Card, Stationery & Gift Industry Gurus www.linkedin.com You could post a message to that group and ask for referrals.

Sign Up for Faire

Faire.com is an online wholesale marketplace that connects independent brands and retailers from around the world. Some reps visit the website to look for new products.

Visit Trade Shows

Trade shows and gift shows are a good place to find reps. These are events where manufacturers (card publishers) display products to prospective buyers (retail stores).

Many of the people staffing booths are sales representatives of the products on display. Some reps are in-house reps (mentioned earlier) working in a booth for one company, and other reps are independent reps that are carrying several artists' lines.

You can usually tell the difference by looking at the booths. Independent reps usually display several very different card lines, often labeled with the artist or publisher's name. An in-house rep will often work in a booth just for one company. Their products might have an overall look and color scheme.

As an artist, you might feel overwhelmed when visiting a trade show, since you are not a buyer or an exhibitor, but I believe it is a good idea to visit at least one show before you start working with reps.

Visiting a trade show can help you understand where you fit in the industry, and it will also show you how different publishers and manufacturers present their products to the public. It is very different from a craft fair.

All shows have special requirements for entry, and in some cases you might be asked to pay a $50 or $100 fee to get it if you are not a store buyer, manufacturer, or sales rep. Most shows are free, but it is usually worth paying a fee, since there are free classes and seminars available throughout the day.

It's possible there is a gift show near you. Here are just a few examples of gift show websites*:

Atlanta Market and More
https://www.atlantamarket.com/

Las Vegas Market and More
https://www.lasvegasmarket.com/

NY Now
https://nynow.com/

Note: Website URLs can often change. Please search online.

As an artist, there are etiquette guidelines you should be aware of when visiting a show. If you want to talk to someone in a booth, don't interrupt a buyer and seller if they are talking. Make sure the booth is somewhat empty before you enter it, and keep your conversation brief. Once you determine the person in the booth is a rep, ask if she ever looks at new lines, and if she does, could you send her samples of your cards. You can request her business card for later contact.

It's helpful to bring greeting card samples, along with a prepared one-sentence description of what your line is about. If she gives you her contact information, it's always good to wait a couple of weeks before contacting her, since reps are often busy processing orders after a show.

If you can't get to any shows because you live too far away, go to any trade show's website, and look for the list of exhibitors. Often, there are several names of sales reps in the exhibitor listings.

Visit Gift Mart Websites

Gift marts are places where manufacturers and sales reps have permanent showrooms year around. They are usually tall office buildings filled with individual booths or rooms. A company usually occupies each room. Unlike gift shows, which only happen a few days each year, a gift mart is a permanent location that store buyers can visit any time of the year. Large manufacturers usually occupy most showrooms, but some rooms are also rented by independent sales reps who display all the lines they carry.

On gift mart websites, all the companies that occupy space in the showroom are listed, and it provides detailed descriptions of the products. If you look closely, you will be able to distinguish large company showrooms from independent sales rep showrooms. Large company showrooms with in-house reps carry a variety of *products* by that company. They tend to describe their showroom offerings as "candles" or "greeting cards." On the other hand, showrooms of independent reps (carrying a variety of artist's lines) tend to emphasize the names of the *artists* or card *companies* they represent. Try to look for showrooms that have many greeting card line names listed. Those are usually the rooms, or the people; you want to make a note of.

Reps who rent showrooms tend to be rep "groups," who are teams of independent reps covering several territories, such as three or four states, or large metropolitan areas such as Los Angeles.

Gift marts are not generally open to the public. The best way to visit one is to go with a friend who owns a business, or ask the show management if you can have a visitor's pass for a day. If you live near a metropolitan area, you probably have a gift mart in your city. Here are sample list of gift mart showroom websites*:

AmericasMart
AMC, Inc. / AmericasMart Atlanta
240 Peachtree Street N.W., Suite 2200
Atlanta, GA 30303
404.220.3000
www.americasmart.com

Dallas Market Center
2100 Stemmons Freeway
Dallas, TX 75207
214-655-6100
dallasmarketcenter.com

Denver Merchandise Mart
451 East 58th Avenue, Suite 4270,
Denver, CO 80216-8470
303-292-6278
www.denvermart.com

LA Mart
1933 South Broadway,
Los Angeles, CA 90007
800.LAMART.4
www.lamart.com

Miami Merchandise Mart
777 NW 72 Avenue
Miami, Florida 33126
305-269-4811
www.miamimerchandisemart.com

Minneapolis Gift Mart
10301 Bren Road West,
Minnetonka, MN 55343
952-932-7200
www.mplsmart.com

New York Market Center
230 Fifth Avenue,
New York, NY 10001
800-698-5617
www.230fifthave.com

If you cannot go to a showroom, you can often find a list of the companies on their website.

Note: Website URLs can often change. Please search online.

Put an Ad in Industry Media Outlets

The greeting card and gift industry have many trade magazines. They offer retail news, and feature new products. These publications often have a section where you can place an ad, and let people in the industry know you are seeking a rep. Even if you don't want to buy an ad, these publications are valuable reading material to learn more about the industry.

Here are several publications dedicated to the greeting card and gift industry.*

Balloons & Parties
65 Sussex Street
Hackensack, NJ 07601
www.balloonsandparties.com

Christian Retailing
600 Rinehart Road
Lake Mary, FL 32746
www.christianretailing.com

GiftBeat
72 Tappan Road
Harrington Park, NJ 07640
www.giftbeat.com

Gift Shop Magazine
195 Hanover Street
Hanover, MA 02339
www.giftshopmag.com

Gifts & Decorative Accessories
360 Park Avenue South
New York, NY 10010
www.giftsanddec.com

Greetings Today
Nashville, 1 Church Gates
Wilderness, Berkhamsted
Herts, HP4 2UB

United Kingdom
www.greetingstoday.co.uk

License! Global Magazine
641 Lexington Avenue
New York, NY 10022
www.licensemag.com

Museums & More
PO Box 128
Sparta, MI 49345
www.museumsandmore.com

Print Magazine
38 East 29th Street, 3rd Floor
New York, NY 10016
www.printmag.com

Party & Paper Retailer
PO Box 128
Sparta, MI 49345
www.partypaper.com

Max Publishing
United House, North Road
London N7 9DP
United Kingdom
https://www.pgbuzz.net/

Stationery Trends Magazine
PO Box 128
Sparta, MI 49345

https://stationerytrends.com/magazine/

Souvenirs, Gifts & Novelties Magazine
10 E. Athens Avenue, #208
Ardmore, PA 19003
www.sgnmag.com

Note: Website URLs can often change. Please search online.

If you decide to place an ad in a publication, you might write up a blurb that looks something like this, (using our earlier example of the "New York Pets" greeting card line).

"Everybody loves a pet! New York Pets is a humorous greeting card line seeking sales reps in California and Nevada. Line generates consistent repeat orders and offers a 20% commission. For more information, visit www.website.com or call Betty at 555-567-5555."

The key information I suggest you include for a trade industry ad is:

- A tagline that represents your card line. (Everybody loves a pet!).

- A unique description of your cards. (New York Pets is a humorous greeting card).

- The territory you need covered (Line generates consistent repeat orders).

- Information about your sales. (Line generates

consistent repeat orders).

- The commission for the sales rep (20% commission).

- Contact information, both active (they can call you) and passive (they can look at your website).

Visit the Greeting Card Association Website

The Greeting Card Association (GCA) sometimes provides news and information for greeting card manufacturers and in the past has even published support materials for marketing greeting cards. https://www.greetingcard.org/

Collect Rep Names

Early on, it helps to collect rep names, even if you aren't ready to contact them. Things you might want to make a note of are:

- Their name.
- Their business name.
- Their business address.
- Their telephone and fax numbers.
- Their email.
- Their website, facebook or LinkedIn profile address.
- The state, city and territory they cover (important).

Later, when you are ready to work with a rep, you will have an available list to contact.

CHAPTER 6
REP READINESS CHECKLIST

There are many things an artist can do before contacting a rep, but I am listing the most important ones.

If you have accomplished the following tasks, I believe you can probably start working with a rep.

You have about fifty different card designs.

While some reps will look at smaller card lines, the odds are better if you have a large assortment.

You have store accounts.

Try to get a handful of store accounts on your own, where your cards are being reordered. You don't want to approach a rep if your cards are not selling.

You are making a profit.

(See Pricing and Profits, Chapter 3)

You have cards already in stock.

Ideally, have at least 100 cards of each card design before talking to a rep. If you have 50 designs, that would be 5,000 cards.

If you feel nervous about printing 5,000 cards, then make sure you know you can manufacture them quickly if you get a large order.

If your new rep faxes you a $1,000 order, can you fill it and ship it out this week?

You have backup suppliers.

Running out of supplies is a serious problem. Make sure you have *second sources* for supplies. If you run out of cellophane bags, it may take two weeks to get more shipped to you.

All businesses can have supply problems, but you don't want to start your relationship with a new rep by *involving her* in your supply problems.

Putting Together a Home Office

Putting an office together can involve filing systems, zoning licenses, and checking accounts. This kind of information is easily available from any basic business book. I am only mentioning it, because it is important and something to consider before working with a rep.

You Have Looked at Business Software

QuickBooks is a software program that is helpful in manufacturing businesses. You can take a local adult school class to explore the program before you buy it. It will keep track of your accounts and generate invoices. It also keeps a historical record of orders, and tracks inventory. Don't feel like you must learn the whole program before you use it, but as your business grows, you will need to move beyond keeping records in a notebook or as one artist described her experience of "trying to find elusive bits of paper."

Consider Different Kinds of "Back-Up" Protection.

On several occasions, I've found it helpful to keep a paper copy of orders received and shipped "just in case" I had to regenerate data.

If someone snatches your computer or your hard drive fails, having a paper trail will allow you to recreate financial information such as: how much money a store owes you and the amount of money you owe your reps. And do you have a paper copy of your art? Or has it disappeared in the digital crash?

Some people rely on external hard drives for their backups, but I prefer storing data remotely in the "cloud." If there is a fire, earthquake or flood, your data is safely stored offsite. Some services, such as Google, Apple and Dropbox offer small amounts of free online storage. You might use this temporarily for urgent sensitive data, but eventually it might be easier to back up your whole computer offsite.

Remote cloud storage is nice because it automatically runs in the background on your computer and you don't have to do anything. And it can cost as little as $5-$10 a month.

I recommend two storage services that I found to be user-friendly: Backblaze www.backblaze.com and Crashplan www.crashplan.com .

What I like the most about them is that they offer something called "versioning." It allows you to go back in time and get 100 different versions of the same document at different stages of editing. There are many times I have overwritten data or art without realizing it. Then a week later, I found the original error and needed the 9:00 o'clock version of the document (and not the 10:00, 11:00 or 12:00 versions). With versioning, I can easily go back to a particular time and date, before the error occurred, and download the uncorrupted version of the file.

Fax Machine?

To fax or not to fax? While technology has moved forward and very few people use fax machines anymore, it might surprise you that some sales reps send their orders by fax. This is because they often write up an order by hand in a store with their own business forms. If you still have that fax machine in the garage, don't toss it quite *yet*.

Support Materials

It helps to provide a rep with support materials, such as a catalog, price sheet and ordering information. If all you can do is give her a one-page flier of your best designs, that's better than nothing, but eventually you should create some type of printed document of your designs. Reps often give these to store buyers, so they can review them when they have time to ponder.

Ready to Ship?

It is easy to buy boxes at the office supply store when you first start out, but they can be expensive when you need a lot. It's better to buy in bulk from a manufacturer who sells boxes in lots of 25. They are about half the price of the office supply store.

Free shipping supplies can be ordered from UPS, USPS and FEDEX, but be aware that these boxes often require you to pay prime shipping rates. You will need to do research and see what pricing works for you.

When packing boxes, it's helpful to use extra padding around the card corners because you don't want them to get dinged or bent. I found that by wrapping several dozen cards together like a brick worked just fine. I put the brick in a box and stuff shipping paper around it, so that the corner of the cards never touched the box.

Money

Do you have enough money in the bank to pay your rep commissions before the store pays you? Usually reps are paid 30 days after you ship the order (independent of whether you received a store payment). Some reps are willing to receive payment after the store pays you, but I prefer paying reps earlier rather than later.

As a rule of thumb, I would make sure you have at least $1,000 available for cash flow when you first start out. As your orders increase, and checks start arriving, then you can gradually increase your cash flow amount.

Time

It helps to set aside at least 20 hours per week for your business, especially when starting out. You want enough time to follow through on shipping orders in 1-5 days after receiving them.

~

If you are able to accomplish most of these tasks before you work with a rep, it will make your experience of running your business much easier and rewarding, and you can avoid unexpected emergencies.

CHAPTER 7
PITCHING YOUR LINE TO A REP

Before contacting a rep to ask them to carry your line, try to find out what they require of new artists. Some reps expect an artist to have several accounts already. Some reps might only want to carry cards with a specific style or subject matter, such as handmade, religious, or humor themes.

When you are ready to pitch your line to a rep, here are some guidelines that might increase your chances of making a good impression.

Find out if they are looking at new lines.

The first time you contact a rep by phone or email, it is always good to ask: *are you looking for new lines?* Rather than *will you look at MY line?* This takes pressure off the rep. They might be busy and don't have time to give you attention. They might have more pressing responsibilities at the moment, than evaluating a new card line.

If they are not looking at new lines, you might ask: *Is there a certain time of year you look at new lines?* If there is, make a note of it and contact them later.

Sometimes a rep will say: "*I'm not looking at new lines, but what kind of line do you have?*"

In a conversation like this, it helps to have a short, clear description of your card line. This description might include your art style (collage?), message (humor?) theme (pets?) and sales history.

Here are some examples of how you might describe a card line in a few sentences. If possible, give them some information on their sales.

"*I have a letterpress line of retro images with unusual mechanical tools, bikes and housewares. I mix these with contemporary sentiments. This line does well in kitchen supply stores.*"

"*My cards have cartoon art with women saying snarky things about their romantic life. These are especially hot sellers on Valentine's Day*"

"*I have a humor line, based on what pets say about humans. My best sellers are cat birthday cards.*"

Give reps your numbers

Reps like numbers.
If you want a rep to pick up your line, the most important

thing you can offer them are your numbers. Things they like to know are:

- The number of cards in your line.
- How many stores you already sell to.
- Your average order amount (in dollars).
- The number and frequency of your reorders so far.
- How long you've been in business.

Reps are in the sales business, so even if they love your cards, they may not think they will sell. Show them any sales statistics that might inspire confidence that your product will make money.

Send Samples

For a sales rep to pick up your line, you have to find a way for them to see your cards. This can be done by mailing them samples, by sending digital images through email, or by encouraging a rep to visit your website.

I believe you increase your odds of getting a rep to pick up your line if they have the opportunity to touch and hold your cards.

Ask Before Sending Samples

Reps often discourage artists from sending unsolicited card samples. They usually have an office full of greeting cards and do not want more cluttering up their workspace. Nor do they want the burden or cost of returning samples to you, if you mistakenly expected that.

Out of courtesy, it is nice to ask the sales rep ahead of time if it is OK to send samples that *don't* need to be returned.

Physical Samples vs. Virtual Samples

If a rep is looking at new card lines, encourage them to allow you to send physical samples in the mail, instead of brochures or website links.

There are two advantages of this: If a rep has samples of your cards in her office, she will be reminded of your line. She might also grab your samples on her way out the door, and show them to a store to see what they think.

Disadvantages of Sending Reps to Your Website

While having a website is important, and many reps say they'd rather look at it than receive cards, I don't believe this is the best way to present the line. Here's why:

• Websites often display a limited amount of cards on one page, and since the average time anyone spends on a website is three minutes, she is less likely to look at the entire website if she does not like the homepage.

• Images on websites are usually small and cards are hard to see, and if they *are* large, sometimes this can cause the webpage to load slower.

• From my experience, it's much faster to flip through a sample deck of cards and pick out the ones I like, rather than negotiate a website and print out specific images.

- You might know exactly where everything is on your website, but a rep might find it confusing to find where the birthday, Christmas and Thank You cards are located.

- Websites cannot properly reflect textures, paper thickness, elegant cards sealed in cellophane, or accurate matching of printed colors.

- A rep cannot open a card on a website to read what's inside. Some artists try to resolve this problem by having two images for each card on the website (front and inside), but that can lead to additional clicks and webpage refreshing. It is much easier to just pick up a card and open it.

- If a rep wants to show your cards to one of her accounts, she will have to print out the images.

- Most people look at websites on small mobile devices instead of desktop computers. This makes your cards look even smaller and harder to read.

- If you have not optimized your site for mobile devices, your cards can look distorted on the screen.

Sending Card Images through Email

If the rep still does not want samples mailed to them, but they are willing to look at digital images, send your images *by email*. This is better than sending them to your website for the following reasons:

- When you email anyone, there is a better chance they will open it and read it, whereas nothing guarantees they will take the time to visit your website.

- In an email, you can choose what images they see first. On a website, you don't know where they will go. So, for example, if you want to feature your top dozen sellers, you can put them all in your email so it doesn't require them to navigate through several web pages to find these cards. You can also put cards in specific order in an email (by top sellers, seasonal, themes, etc,).

- By sending each card image as a separate image file in your email (which is different than reducing them to put on a one page 8.5-by-11 inch flier), reps can print out the ones they like and toss rest. This will save them ink and digital storage space. If possible, scan the card images instead of photographing them. Then you can avoid lighting issues and blurred text.

- Avoid sending images in a PDF format unless the rep requests it. Sometimes these can be hard to preview in an email because they have to be downloaded first. Also, some people do not have the correct software to open a PDF file.

- Avoid sending your images inside of a digital "folder." Instead, embed the images directly into your email message, so when the rep opens the email, the cards are sitting under your text. You can also write comments above or below a card, such as

"Here are my twelve top sellers" and "Here are my birthday cards."

- Try to keep your email file size under 1 to 2 MG total. It is better to send twenty images at low resolution than ten at high resolution.

- A good rule of thumb is to send files that are 72 dpi and 500 pixels wide. This way, if the rep wants to print images out, they are large enough to look like a greeting card, yet small enough to be easily stored without using up a lot of hard drive space.

- When preparing your digital images, you can make smaller file sizes (and fit more in one email) by using the SAVE FOR WEB & DEVICES function in Photoshop instead of the SAVE AS option under the file menu.

All of these digital tips above are suggestions for making a good impression when you first contact a rep that does not know you. If you follow these guidelines, I believe it will increase the odds that your designs will be seen, you will get a response, and ideally the rep will pick up your line.

Mailing Samples

If a rep encourages you to mail card samples, here are some helpful tips for preparing the samples, and what to put in the box.

- Put reference codes on the back of each card, such as

#1, #2, #3, etc. Reps expect all cards to have a code, either pre printed or handwritten on the back. You should have a different code for each design. For example, if you have a card line of 50 different kinds of flower images, you need to assign a code to each one. When reps write orders, they need to know #45 is the red rose card.

• Include a price sheet. Clearly specify your wholesale price and retail prices, both for dozens and half dozens. Cards are normally sold in packets of 6 and 12 of one design. A typical store order might be 1/2 dozen of 12 designs (or 72 cards).

• Include a catalog or brochure of your card line. This could be something as simple as a brochure created on your home office printer.

• Include information about your business, such as stores you currently sell to, your experience or skills.

~

The best thing you can offer a rep is a product *that sells for them*, and not a product you want them *to sell for you*.

In the same way, getting your cards in a store and seeing them on a rack is a great accomplishment, but for a rep, that is only the first step of their larger goal, which is to get reorders.

CHAPTER 8
WORKING WITH REPS

Every rep works a little differently, and over time I've seen that is a benefit of the career. They have the freedom to run their own business in a way that fits their lifestyle.

As a manufacturer, you might want to know how to evaluate a potential rep to see if it's a good fit.

You may prefer to work with a rep that carries a limited amount of lines. Or perhaps you want a rep that is willing to exhibit at trade shows. Rarely did I ever work with a rep who I felt was a bad match, and if I did, we usually parted ways easily with no hard feelings

Since most reps don't require contracts, it makes it easy to move on if either of you want to.

Things you might want to ask a rep:

- What territories do you serve?
  This is probably the most important question to ask a rep. You should avoid overlapping any territories that would cause two reps to call on the same store (more on that later).

- How many lines do you carry?
  A rep might carry anywhere from 20 to 100 lines (artists/manufacturers). If a rep carries too many lines, your product may fall between the cracks and never get attention; but then again, if only 30% of their products are greeting cards (and perhaps the other 70% are gifts), you may get more attention by being one of a few card lines.

- How many accounts (stores) do you have?
  Every rep has a territory. A rep in a less populated area tends to travel more and have fewer accounts, than a rep in an urban area. You might have only two reps for the entire state of New Mexico, but as many as seven reps just for the metropolitan area of Los Angeles. Reps who cover less populated areas tend to have fewer accounts.

- What kind of lines do you currently carry?
  If your rep specializes in jewelry and you are the only card line they carry, this could be a bad match if she only visits jewelry stores. This rep will probably not make a special trip to a stationery store just to show your card line. On the other hand, if the rep

only carries cards and all the lines are similar to yours, this, too, may be a bad match. Try to find a rep that carries lines that are complementary, yet different from yours.

- Do you go to trade shows?
Some sales reps attend trade shows and set up booths to display their lines. You may have the opportunity to have your cards in a show. Reps may ask the artist for a $50 to $500 contribution for exhibitor booth fees (depending on the square footage of the booth, and how much space your line covers).

It's nice to contribute to the booth fees because reps pay thousands of dollars for a booth with no guarantees their sales will cover their costs. It's a reasonable request to ask manufacturers to help out with costs. If you do not want to contribute to a booth, then you should not expect your products to be displayed at the show.

You can always be upfront with a rep and tell her what your budget is. If you can only pay $100, perhaps she can adjust the size of the space in the booth for you.

- How much is your average order?
If you have an estimate of how many orders a rep will generate, this will help you plan a monthly budget for income and expenses. It is also useful information if you need to evaluate how your line is doing, compared to what reps predicted.

Contracts

I have found that independent reps rarely ask for you to sign a contract (although rep "groups" can vary on this). Even without a contract, it is advisable to write down your own business policies and give them a copy. If there is confusion about commission rates or shipping costs, you can refer back to the information you gave to them.

I encourage artists to make an informal "Agreement Form." The agreement form can be more like an informational sheet, rather than a legal contract. For example, one of my policies was that I did not accept returns. For some reps, this might be a surprise. It is better they know this up front, instead of finding out later, after they accept a return from a store.

I requested the agreement to be signed and faxed back to me before I shipped any card samples or catalogs. Requesting this usually guaranteed that they read the form, and it didn't get lost on a pile of papers on a desk.

An agreement form might include the following:

- Territory: Name the territory the rep will cover.

- Prices: List wholesale prices of your cards in dozens and half dozens, and if there is any discount for larger quantities.

- Commission: State what commission you pay. Usually it is in the range of 20%.

- Payday: Name the day of the month the rep is paid. I

made it a policy to pay reps two weeks after the prior month. For example, their commission for all the orders I shipped in May would be paid on June 15th.

• Minimum orders: Say what your minimum size order is. A good starting point is $100, but it is OK to not have a minimum. This might allow a store to try out your line first, without investing a large amount of money.

• Returns: Say whether you accept returns, and on what conditions. For example, you might accept undamaged holiday card returns.

• Promotional materials: List what sales support you offer, such as catalogs, store signs or store racks.

• Late accounts: Explain what you will do if an account is 90 days overdue in paying. Reps like to know if a store is way overdue. Maybe the store is struggling for some reason. Reps will often help you collect, if a store is really late.

• Rack programs: Do you offer a rack program? This describes the kind of card racks you offer. You may not need this at the beginning of your business, but later, offering racks to stores is a good idea for increasing sales.

• Shipping charges: Are your charges by weight or by a percentage of the invoice? I chose to have a percentage of the invoice, so that even the rep could estimate the shipping charges at a sales meeting.

Whose job is it anyway?

Sometimes it is hard to know where to draw the line between the artist's job and the rep's job. For me, an easy rule of thumb was: The artist should not be communicating with the store.

If there is a question on an order, the artist should call the rep and not call the store.

If the artist starts calling stores, it can interfere with the rep's role.

Here is a typical example of a potential conflict:

Event: A store calls you (the artist) and leaves you a message saying they want to order more cards. You call them back and take an order over the phone and forget to tell the rep. You didn't realize the rep already had an appointment to show your card, and she makes a special trip to the store the following week. She discovers you already made an order over the phone, *and* your order was half the amount she believes she could have generated.

Solution: Instead of calling the store back, contact the rep as soon as possible and ask them to follow through on the new order.

Goal: You want the store to rely on the rep for customer service and communication.

Why: If you allow stores to order directly from you, it will create more work for everyone, you will probably receive a smaller order, and it will confuse the rep.

If an artist takes a phone order directly from store, some problems can develop:

- More Work
  It will take you more time to process an order because you will have to contact two people: The rep and the store instead of one (the rep). You will need to give the rep a copy of the order.

  You might accidentally write the order incorrectly if the store does not have the proper ordering codes in front of them. They may try to verbally describe the cards by the way they look.

  Phone orders can also turn into larger tasks if they request additional things, like mailing a catalog.

- Lost Appointments
  As mentioned in the example above, you may be unaware of a prior appointment the rep had with the store. Perhaps the rep was going to drop by that store tomorrow to deliver catalogs, and take an order. If you took the order over the phone, the rep has less incentive to even go to the store now. Then catalogs are not delivered, missing envelopes are not replaced, and racks are not straightened.

- You Get Smaller Orders
  If you have limited sales skills, you will probably

generate a smaller order if you take it by phone from the store, than if the rep does. It is my experience that reps can sell more cards than I could.

• You Disrupt Her Sales Plan
If you take orders directly from the store, you might interfere with a rep's sales strategy. Some reps have specific sales calendars where they show all their Valentine's cards on a certain date. If a store orders all their Valentine's cards for the season from you, it can undermine the rep's overall plan for other artists they represent.

• Unexpected Agreements
If a store orders from you, they might request extra perks the rep is uncomfortable with. For example, if you agree to a discount, that will affect the rep's commission.

Always encourage the store to call the rep instead of you. Or contact the rep yourself. It makes a lot less work for everyone. This does not mean you should hang up the phone if a store calls you. Just explain that you do not normally process direct orders, but you will do it this once time. And *always* let the rep know you took the order, and send them a copy.

In my opinion, once you start working with sales reps, it is disrespectful to take orders directly from a store unless it is an emergency (rack is completely empty) or the rep is on vacation. You don't want a rep showing up to an appointment with your card line, expecting to make a sale, only to have the store buyer say "oh, I just ordered those cards from the artist the other day." It wastes the rep's time and can cause friction between the rep and artist. Also, the rep may have driven many miles to a store appointment.

Most importantly, a rep receives the commission no matter who took the order. Reps are paid for any orders generated in their territory, even if they are on vacation. An artist might think "But *I* took this order, therefore I deserve the commission." However, the rep has already earned the commission because she does more than write orders. Most of what reps do, an artist never sees, such straightening card racks and replacing lost envelopes.

On the other hand, if you find a store complaining a lot, saying the rep never calls back, this is a problem. Try to find out what is going on. Is your rep fulfilling your expectations? Or is the store a difficult business to work with? You need to figure out which one it is.

Sometimes you might find yourself in a situation where there is a conflict between a store and a rep. I tend to err on the side of supporting the rep's preferences, especially if I have worked with them for several years and trust their judgment.

An example of this might be: Two competitive stores near each other want to buy your cards. Since it is standard policy that reps do not sell to stores near each other, someone needs to decide which store can carry your cards. The store that is *not* chosen will probably be unhappy about it.

I like to let the rep decide what store they prefer to work with, even if it means a smaller order for me. Usually reps have good reasons for their store preferences. Perhaps they know that a store is slow at paying bills, or has been in business for a short time. By relying on the rep's judgment, it allows them the freedom to make decisions on your behalf.

Reps are people-persons, and tend to be peacemakers. More often than not, if a problem arises, the rep has already invested many hours trying to resolve it, long before you even hear about it.

Territories

Reps work by geographic territories and it is the responsibility of the artist to make sure *no two territories overlap.* For example, if you have a rep that covers northern New Hampshire, and another one that covers southern New Hampshire, make sure you know where the division is between them, and check with both of them.

A simple way to keep track of territories is to purchase a spiral bound book called the *United States Zip Code* atlas. It has detailed maps of each state, and you can photocopy individual maps and ask each rep to outline the territory they cover.

Territories tend to be separated by population, and not necessarily by state. A northern California rep might cross the Nevada border to sell in Lake Tahoe because the Nevada rep does not travel that far north. A Chicago rep might dip down into Indiana since the metropolitan area spills over the border.

States with small populations might be covered by only one rep, but densely populated metropolitan areas like New York City, Los Angeles, San Francisco and Chicago who have several reps in small geographical areas, requiring detailed maps. In a case like this, make sure nothing overlaps. Sometimes reps know each other and have already informally agreed to divide their territories on their own. This makes things much easier for you if they know each other and have an understanding, but always remember to still ask them to write down or send them a map and ask them to draw lines where their boundaries are.

Adding Designs

Reps expect the artist to discontinue slow selling cards and replace them with new designs. A good plan is to add new designs 3-4 times a year: January, May and August, along with seasonal items (approximately 6 months ahead of the holiday).

Paying Reps

The best way to show a rep appreciation is to pay them on time. I abide by the motto of "Pay reps before you pay yourself, because without them, I have no business." Some general rules of thumb are:

- Avoid any situation that would cause them to call you and ask for their check.

- Normally, the artist pays the rep once a month for all the prior months' orders (independent of whether the store has paid you). This is referred to as "paying reps by ship date." For example, if the rep sends you ten orders in March, and you ship them all in March, you should pay the rep one check for all those order commissions. But if you receive ten orders in March, and you ship nine in March, and one in April, then you send the rep the commission payment for just nine March orders. The order shipped in April will be paid in the following commission check.

- Some artists pay reps after being paid by a store, but this is not common. Reps like to have a predictable income and it's less paperwork.

- Artists usually pay the rep a 20% commission on the wholesale price of the cards. Therefore, if you receive an order for $200 wholesale (the price you charge the store), the rep's commission will be $40.

- The artist normally pays for card samples, shipping samples and promotional materials, such as brochures and catalogs.

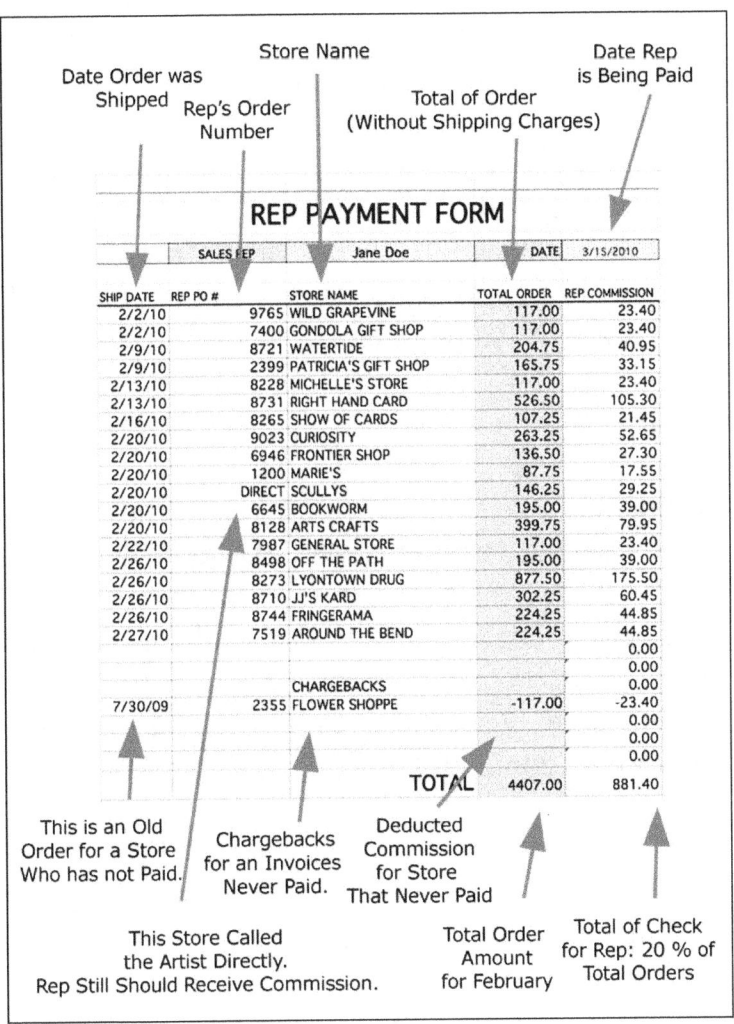

REP PAYMENT FORM

| SALES REP | | Jane Doe | | DATE | 3/15/2010 |

SHIP DATE	REP PO #	STORE NAME	TOTAL ORDER	REP COMMISSION
2/2/10	9765	WILD GRAPEVINE	117.00	23.40
2/2/10	7400	GONDOLA GIFT SHOP	117.00	23.40
2/9/10	8721	WATERTIDE	204.75	40.95
2/9/10	2399	PATRICIA'S GIFT SHOP	165.75	33.15
2/13/10	8228	MICHELLE'S STORE	117.00	23.40
2/13/10	8731	RIGHT HAND CARD	526.50	105.30
2/16/10	8265	SHOW OF CARDS	107.25	21.45
2/20/10	9023	CURIOSITY	263.25	52.65
2/20/10	6946	FRONTIER SHOP	136.50	27.30
2/20/10	1200	MARIE'S	87.75	17.55
2/20/10	DIRECT	SCULLYS	146.25	29.25
2/20/10	6645	BOOKWORM	195.00	39.00
2/20/10	8128	ARTS CRAFTS	399.75	79.95
2/22/10	7987	GENERAL STORE	117.00	23.40
2/26/10	8498	OFF THE PATH	195.00	39.00
2/26/10	8273	LYONTOWN DRUG	877.50	175.50
2/26/10	8710	JJ'S KARD	302.25	60.45
2/26/10	8744	FRINGERAMA	224.25	44.85
2/27/10	7519	AROUND THE BEND	224.25	44.85
				0.00
				0.00
		CHARGEBACKS		0.00
7/30/09	2355	FLOWER SHOPPE	-117.00	-23.40
				0.00
				0.00
				0.00
		TOTAL	4407.00	881.40

Labels around the form:

- Date Order was Shipped
- Rep's Order Number
- Store Name
- Total of Order (Without Shipping Charges)
- Date Rep is Being Paid
- This is an Old Order for a Store Who has not Paid.
- Chargebacks for an Invoices Never Paid.
- Deducted Commission for Store That Never Paid
- This Store Called the Artist Directly. Rep Still Should Receive Commission.
- Total Order Amount for February
- Total of Check for Rep: 20 % of Total Orders

Sample form when mailing reps their commission check.

Adding More Reps

Once you start working with reps, they will be one of your best sources for acquiring additional reps in different territories. It might be surprising that a rep on the west coast knows a rep on the east coast, but since reps work in a unique profession, they are aware of colleagues throughout the United States and beyond. This is because they meet each other at trade shows or have recommended lines to each other in the past. They might also carry the same lines.

Rep Groups

Rep groups are a team of sales reps who all work together to cover a large territory. Usually there is one "principle", or owner of the group, and this person has "sub-reps," or people that work *for* them and get a smaller commission. I have worked with rep groups in my greeting card business and they tend to consist of about six to ten people including the principle.

On the surface, this might sound like a great opportunity to hire a team of reps at all once, but there are pros and cons of rep groups.

Pros

- The group has already divided up their own territory equally, so you do not have to worry about overlapping areas.

- You only have to write one commission check for all

the reps.

• They often have permanent showrooms that will display your cards.

• They tend to exhibit at trade shows, which gives you more exposure.

• They generally have a uniform system and set of policies.

• They tend to have high profile accounts and store chains.

• You can do all your communication through the rep principle, instead of each individual rep.

Cons

• If they drop your line, you lose all the reps at once.

• The sub reps have a high turnover rate. Some of them are trying out a new career and don't realize all the responsibilities involved with being a card rep. They may also lack sales skills.

• My experience is that about half of the sub reps in a group are great sellers, and the other half I may never hear from. This can be disappointing if you have gone to all the trouble of sending out sample decks to the entire group.

• Groups tend to carry a lot of card lines and the

biggest companies tend to take priority over the smaller, independent artists.

• You cannot drop a poor performing sub rep and replace them with someone else. Working with groups is usually an all-or-nothing package.

• Because rep groups often have high staff turnover, this can be frustrating for stores. Typically, one of the first warning signs a group is not working out is when a store calls you and does not even know who their rep is. Ideally, the store should always know this, or at least they should know how to contact the principal (owner) of the group to find out.

Working With Solo Reps

I found my top-selling reps were solo reps who did not work in a group. I'm not sure why this is the case, but I attribute it to their freedom to make independent decisions about what lines they want to carry and what stores they want to service. Members of a rep group do not always have this authority.

Solo reps tend to have many years of experience and long-term relationships with store buyers. This can also be true for the owner of a rep group, but it is less true for their subreps.

When Things Aren't Working

Sometimes you might find when you are first starting out working with a rep, you will only get one order in a month. It is always good to be upfront and ask the rep if anything is wrong. It could be that:

- They have not had enough time to show your line to all their accounts.

- The rep is not showing the line at all. They could be overwhelmed with work, or perhaps they only are showing seasonal items at the moment.

- They are not doing well with your line. Perhaps they are trying hard to sell your cards, but no one is buying them.

- There is something going on in the rep's personal life. I found that when a rep's sales suddenly drop for no reason, something has happened, such as a family member becoming ill.

- They may be carrying too many lines, and cannot give your line the full attention they hoped for.

- They are getting pressured from one of their lines to sell more, and if this is a large company the rep relies on for a significant part of their income, that company requires extra attention. Even if your line sells well, perhaps they need to attend to another manufacturer's issues temporarily.

If you find that months have gone by, and the rep has not sent you any orders, it is important to contact them. They are often relieved to be able to talk about what the problem is. You can say something like "*I noticed we didn't get any orders in June. Is there something I can do to help you?"* It's possible they are busy, and would appreciate some temporary help. Perhaps you can send them some free samples to hand out to stores, or more catalogs.

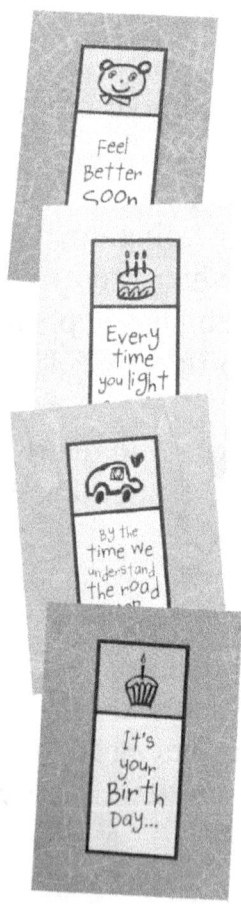

CHAPTER 9
CONCLUSION

Working with sales representatives is enjoyable.

Reps have an upbeat attitude, while also being hard workers. Some have become friends, and I continue to feel fortunate I've had the privilege to know them.

Understanding what reps do, finding the right rep, and learning how to work with them are easy skills to learn, but it's not always clear from the beginning how the manufacturer-rep relationship works. Hopefully this book has touched on some basic tips to help you with that.

Sometimes artists tell me they are discouraged after hitting a bump in the road. Perhaps their line was rejected, or they got unpleasant feedback. Some people convince themselves their goals are not realistic, or are just *too hard*. But often, there are many things they have already done that are much, much harder. Anyone who has raised children, held down a demanding job, acquired a college degree or remodeled a house knows what it takes to be determined, committed, and what to do when faced with difficult challenges. All of these accomplishments require overcoming periodic failures, which are often much harder than taking the leap to try and sell your card designs.

Perhaps part of the reason some artists become discouraged is because they have not found their own cheering section. It helps to have people around you who are invested in your success, and are happy for you.

Having worked in the greeting card industry for years, I still experience unpredictable responses when telling people what I do for a living. They usually blurt out with enthusiasm "I've *always* wanted to do that!" Greeting cards are fun and people enjoy hearing about what you are doing.

I recall a humorous situation in particular when I attended a formal business breakfast and lecture at the Sheraton Palace in down San Francisco. There were about 200 people in a large ballroom, seated at tables of eight. The speaker of the event asked us all to go around the table, introduce ourselves, and say what we did for a living.

As each person at my table described what he or she did, I started to feel out of place. My group was an assortment of attorneys, a financial investor, and business executives. I admit I felt a little intimidated since I had never worked in those environments. When it was my turn to talk, I said "Hi. I'm Kate. I make handmade greeting cards," which caused a few confused looking faces.

I quickly welcomed the mid morning break and made a beeline to the snacks in the back of the room, asking myself: What *was* I doing there? Then two of the people at my table, both attorneys, approached me individually to talk. They said almost the same thing: One described how she always wished she could start a greeting card business. The other said she was counting down the days until retirement, so she could do something fun, like me. Imagine my surprise. Many people have a passion for making cards.

One thing that the greeting card business offers that is hard to find in almost any other job, is: *You get to decide what messages are put out into the world.*

Those messages are packed up in little boxes, picked up by the UPS man, transported across the country, unpacked in stores, bought by customers and given to people in cities, on farms, in hospitals, at weddings, and in transitions. I've stumbled upon my cards in office cubicles, lunchrooms, classrooms and even once a friend bought my card (not realizing it was mine) and sent it to me. That card traveled from coast to coast, and then back again. A complete circle.

Cards touch all kinds of people. I know, because they write to me, and tell me their stories.

There is so much gained by taking chances in life, and so much lost by not trying. So I say: Put your message out into the world. Storm ahead, and enjoy the ride.

~

RESOURCES

Greeting Card Consultants

Here is a list of people I know and recommend for advice and feedback. I've worked with some of them myself.

For latest updates visit kateharperblog.blogspot.com and select link on left for: Consultants.

Ginger McCleskey helps card designers who want their designs evaluated for sales potential. She has been a greeting card sales rep for over 20 years. https://gingermccleskey.com/

Carolyn Edlund works with card designers to understand the industry, create a collection, pricing, and learn sales strategies. www.ArtsyShark.com

Cheryl Phelps teaches classes and helps artists who want to put together a portfolio for licensing. https://www.cherylphelps.com/

Ronnie Walter helps artists who want to license their

cards to publishers. She has worked as an art licensing agent and has designed hundreds of cards and gifts.
www.ronniewalter.com

Social Networks And Peer-To-Peer Advice

Greeting Card Designer Facebook Page
This is a private facebook group for artists, writers and other professionals in the greeting card business. You will need to answer some basic questions on your card design experience and have a website that represents your artwork.
 www.facebook.com/groups/greetingcarddesigner

Recommended Books

Start and Run a Greeting Card Business From a British author, whose country has a long history of greeting card design, she takes you step-by-step through the process of starting and running your business with lots of useful practical advice to help you.

Greeting Card Design This volume features a vast array of fun, elegant, simple and imaginative greeting cards designed by internationally known artists, illustrators and calligraphers.

Pushing the Envelope Written from both the manufacturer and sales rep perspectives, this nuts and bolts guide is full of industry information, sales tips and guidance for building successful and profitable rep relationships. Kate's Note: This book was written by my top selling sales rep in the country.

Greeting Card Design and Illustration This art technique book is a comprehensive and practical guide to all aspects of designing and creating professional greeting cards. Samples of 130 actual greeting cards. leads you through every stage of the design process.

20 Steps to Art Licensing: How to Sell Your Designs to Card and Gift Companies A booklet on how to license your art to companies that publish greeting cards, and manufacture coffee mugs, magnets, wall hangings, kitchen items, and dozens of other gift items. This booklet covers 20 basic steps from how to prepare your art, to what companies to contact. It includes topics on: How to find agents, classes and what trade shows to attend.

You Can Write Greeting Cards This hands-on guide features practical instruction and exercises that teach beginners how to survey the market, find their niche, and write greetings cards that say just the right thing.

7 Mistakes Greeting Card Writers Make Booklet on common mistakes greeting card writers make and what to avoid when submitting greeting card verse to publishers.

How to Write and Sell Greeting Cards, Bumper Stickers, T-Shirts and Other Fun Stuff A successful freelancer shares her years of experience and advice in writing for the "social expression market".

Write Greeting Cards Like a Pro Moore knows the ins and outs of the greeting card business. In this hands-on guide, she offers practical instruction, idea joggers, and exercises that will teach you how to survey the market, find your niche, and write greeting cards that say just the right thing.

The Complete Photo Guide to Cardmaking This book includes step-by-step photographed instructions for a wide range of techniques, as well as projects to accompany each area of card making. All paper-crafting techniques that can be employed for card making are thoroughly covered, including a comprehensive description of paper types available, folding options and techniques, coloring and image transfer methods, and adding embellishments.

The Encyclopedia of Greeting Card Tools and Techniques Featuring hundreds of handmade cards from leading artists, plus step-by-step photographs of key skills.

Creative Lettering: Techniques and Tips from Top Artists Sixteen calligraphers, painters, collagists, card makers, fiber artists, and graphic designers—give their personal perspectives on lettering. They all offer their favorite tools, how they use them, their signature technique with step-by-step instructions and photos, and an alphabet sampler of their own font.

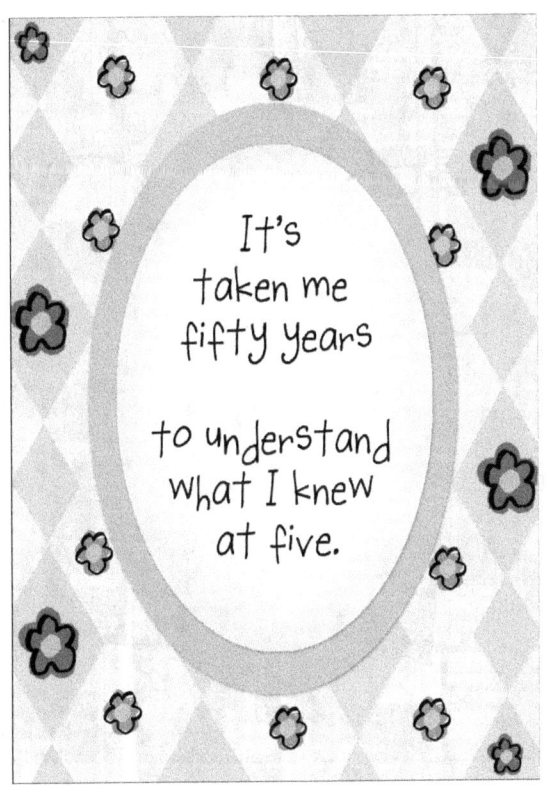

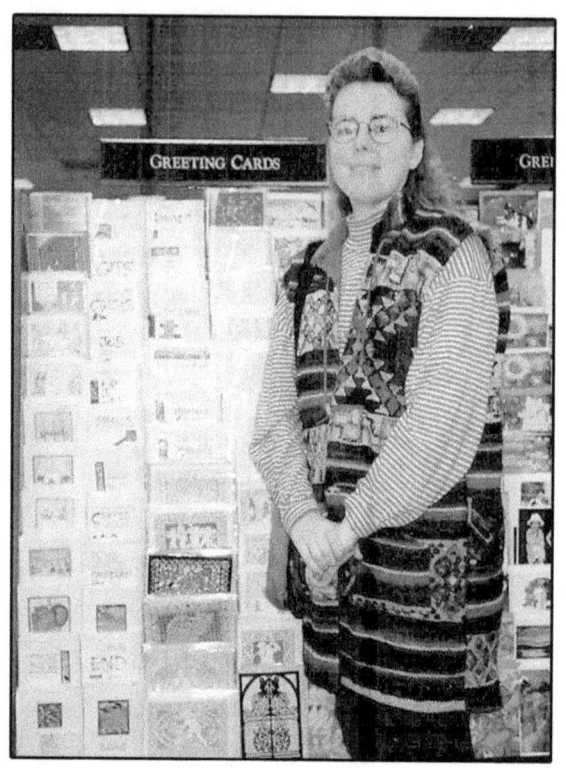

ABOUT THE AUTHOR

Kate Harper is a greeting card and gift designer in Berkeley, California. She has designed over a thousand gifts, greeting cards, magnets, t-shirts, coasters, placemats, rubber stamps, coffee mugs, paper pads, and embroidery kits.

Kate Harper

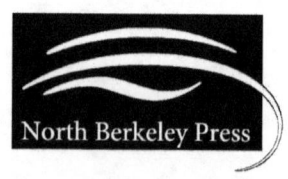

www.kateharperdesigns.com

www.ingramcontent.com/pod-product-compliance
Lightning Source LLC
Chambersburg PA
CBHW071230170526
45165CB00003B/1059